PHANTOM NUMBER:

AN ABECEDARIUM FOR APRIL

Phantom Number: An Abecedarium for April, is a courageous exploration of motherhood, culture and grief, within worlds charged by both beauty and inequity. There are more questions here than answers. Observations and revelations are intimately drawn from this author's life. The work is elegiac, a song of mourning. It is a "Family Portrait with the Missing." But those who are missing (and missed) are not left to "an absent beyond." Those who have died are joined by (H)istory and a profound care that moves the poems out of lamentation alone and into broader purpose: connection. Between the living, the dead, the sorrowful, the farm, the sidewalk, the stars, Ulmer has a sweeping sensibility that takes in the below and above in surprising and equal measure. Yes, this is an abecedarium, which some may find too fixed, but this work is not at all staid, it is as dynamic as a son's wonder, a mother's search for answers, or a friend's generosity. This abecedarian is used to haunting effect, and how better to consider the child's questions that will eventually lead to adult understandings? How better to keep us remembering the beginning as we each approach each respective end, and ask ourselves "What It Means to Continue." *My son and I walk and walk. Whenever we come across anything dead (mouse, worm, bird), we dig a hole for it—* Read Ulmer's insightful work of startlement and it may move you out of denial into pain, yes, but also, precious possibility.

—Vievee Francis, author of *Forest Primeval*

With what language, with what music, can we speak to our dead? In Spring Ulmer's *Phantom Number* this impossible, aching question is addressed again and again through heartbreaking, powerful poems that nonetheless refuse to settle for elegy, refuse to rest in longing or fear, though April, the beloved friend, is gone. Instead, this book-length abecedarian insists on the *and, and, and* of life itself. The constraint of the alphabet feels urgent, as if without that structure, it would all overwhelm and overflow, all get away. For as much as this is a book loaded with grief and righteous rage, it is even more a book holding on to life, demanding life, almost dizzy with sensation and love for all that remains, the child, most of all, but also the "inconceivable beauty" in the fragile, temporary, and miraculous everything: ant, bat, cloud, dream, all for April, all for us, the readers, in our precarious and precious now.

—Julie Carr, author of *Underscore*

It's a loaded deck, we all know that. Yet when we speak of power in poems, we're often too careful, as if trying to secretly unload the dice, to slowly diffuse the bomb in the spray of the blast, mimes to the stillness of an aftermath. Meantime Spring Ulmer's work draws its pressure—circular, irregular as flung bats—as if directly from the whirlwind itself. But, even in elegy, in grief, in fury flown inward, and outward, these aren't metaphysical poems. Instead, as if boomeranged by the thrust from ruptures in social contracts and natural rhythms alike, we're met, poem after poem, and line by line, with a contending force, a vital animation that moves, and moves us, according to metabolisms, lyrical, which can't be predicted, traced, or policed. So much and so many of the living are already gone; ok. Spring Ulmer calls up the needed-beloved who are left, and some who left, to come on over and cut the deck. Let's deal: "here we are—"... "What does it mean that everything keeps barreling on?"

—Ed Pavlic, author of *Let's Let that Are Not Yet: Inferno*

THE DORSET PRIZE FOR POETRY

Poem as wish for a phone that can talk to the dead. As text sent into the ether, unanswered. Elegiac alphabet book of love and heartache etched with the words of poets, philosophers, activists, and heroes, from Lucille Clifton to Birdie Africa, child survivor of the MOVE bombing, from Darnella Frazier, who videotaped the George Floyd murder, to Walter Benjamin and Zakiyyah Iman Jackson. And always the revenant and soul at the epicenter, poet, essayist, teacher, and friend April Freely, "killed by racism, age 38—," the April of the book's title. "April died and moths emerged / and ate up all the green— / April in a casket (skin grey)— / April's yellow dress sways—." April, who speaks in enjambments. April, modifier and sieve, who calls forth and transfigures history, philosophy, environmental disaster, racism, activism, motherhood, language, friendship, and loss. "I wish I knew where to put the grief. There is nothing; no gutter. Everything floods. The confusion is even nature's own," Spring Ulmer writes. The organizing principle, lest the lyric gush over the edge of the page, is the forward motion of the alphabet, and the adamant litanies that spring from it, sometimes epic, at other times, miniaturized. Spring Ulmer has managed to compose a voluminous collection from fragments that cohere into a fluent, many-voiced oratorio, and "the grand narrative that is myth." Yet for all its intellectual breadth and perceptual prowess, I love this book for its intimacy. Maybe it is the truth of all lyric poetry, that in the echo of the grieved-for, we come to know the griever.

—Judge's Citation by Diane Seuss, author of *frank: sonnets*

Spring Ulmer is the author of *Benjamin's Spectacles* (selected by Sonia Sanchez for Kore Press's 2007 First Book Award), *The Age of Virtual Reproduction*, *Bestiality of the Involved*, and *Phantom Number: An Abecedarium for April* (selected by Diane Seuss as the winner of Tupelo Press's 2022 Dorset Prize). She lives in upstate New York with her son.

PHANTOM NUMBER:

AN ABECEDARIUM FOR APRIL

SPRING ULMER

TUPELO PRESS
NORTH ADAMS, MA

Phantom Number: An Abecedarium for April

Copyright © 2025 Spring Ulmer. All rights reserved.

ISBN-13: 978-1-961209-17-6
Library of Congress Control Number: 2024044679
Design by Allison O'Keefe

Cover Art: Jennifer Packer, "A Stone's Throw", 2021, Oil on canvas.
April Freely (1982-2021), sitter. By permission of the artist, courtesy of
Sikkema Jenkins & Co., New York.

First paperback edition: February 2025

Tupelo Press
P.O. Box 1767
North Adams, Massachusetts 01247
(413) 664-9611 / Fax: (413) 664-9711
editor@tupelopress.org / www.tupelopress.org

Tupelo Press is an award-winning independent literary press that
publishes fine fiction, non-fiction, and poetry in books that are a joy
to hold as well as read. Tupelo Press is a registered 501(c)(3) non-profit
organization, and we rely on public support to carry out our mission
of publishing extraordinary work that may be outside the realm of the
large commercial publishers. Financial donations are welcome and are
tax deductible.

...there is a place
behind the place
of nothingness

—Sohrab Sepehri

For April Freely

Contents

I Need a Phone

—Phones for sale! Phones for sale! Phones for sale! Two little phones—

—I need a phone that can talk to the dead.

—They can talk to bats. Two little bat phones for sale! Two little bat phones for sale!

Zakiyyah Iman Jackson Lays It Out

...genes never act alone but always 'in concert' with social and environmental partners—

...in a racialized system, to delay or avoid death from disease requires something in excess of technological innovation and even equitable access.to medical care; it requires symbolic capital—

...race resides...in the (im)material effects of interactional systems—

...racism introduces dangerous amounts of inflammation into the body, increasing black women's 'allostatic load' or the 'wear and tear' on the body that occurs when exposed to a stressor—

...to broaden our conception of politics—and by politics, I mean war—to include gross health-related inequities—

Don't Be Dead I Love You So

A bird calls with four, short, monotone bursts—
A bird rises up out of a tree—
A black streak of mold runs up the tree's trunk—
A blood clot, died of a blood clot—
A brokenness that is also a blackness—

A Ghost Says: Go and Tell the World What You Have Seen

A funeral—
A magazine page on the wall that reads, *Have You Lost the Spring in Your Step?*
A man holds the bloody leg and hoof of a goat—
A man walks a clump of grass on a leash—
A dinosaur embryo, head tucked—
A mass of bones—
A mother who performs backbreaking labor—

A Child's Notebook

[The earth is] *a nis place, really nis. Trees grow—*

A Phone Rings

A phantom number—

UNMOORED

A pile of gravel this high—
A pine slab—
A place in the middle of a wood—
A snowflake sticker on the back end of the boom truck—
A soft bat suit with inflated arm and leg wings—
A stone letter—
A translucent pepper you can hide in sauce—
A way of life—
A wild bouquet—

After April

Above the industrial pit,
children haul banana
leaves, yellowed, behind
them, as if dragging giant
tails. It's raining hearts.
Fat, one bursts open—

After a detective discovered April's body—
After a line by Lucille Clifton—
After I walked out into summer
and fell into my mom's arms—
After sundown, stars' tail ends fall off—

Agamben writes, *[R]acism alone*
can justify the murderous function of the State—

All the gourds drying—
All the rotten seed heads winded, enlightened—
An impossible address—
An insect's breath is to the earth's
breath: one and the same—

And cut out—
And her [April's] voice—
And how she lost it to this nation
amidst a display of fireworks—
And it fucks with me; my son is calling
out for me—
[April would call]
and say, *Just to hear your voice—*

A Poet's Life

And sticky feet, the cicada (molt stuck in sap)—
And that silver sugar (bowl)—
And the fear that I was sick, my son was sick—
And the pain in April's leg—
And the siren speaks for her—
And the unaccountable—
And totally lost—
And yet blood still flows
from a 30,000-year-old
mammoth (named Buttercup)?

Animals move through air or water, creating
vortices or whorls that then form a wake—
Anxiety at night that I will die, abandon my child—

April died and moths emerged
and ate up all the green—
April in a casket (skin grey)—
April's yellow dress sways—
Army ants swarm, volunteering
their own bodies—
Around the casket (arteries pump)—
As bridges other ants cross over—

Ash Pours Down the Chimney

Backwards days—

Bats fly above dark land, pushing off
the roof like skateboarders push off the lip
of a ramp, barely resting there, before
swooping, arcing, circling back—

Bats, four or more above the dark land—

Before capitalism, everything was nature—

Bye!

Bent alongside the event horizon—
Besotted by buttercups—
Black ink spills—
Black squares copied again and again (faceless veils)—
Black women develop fibroids at four times the rate of white women—
Bleed—
Bled—
Blow—
Bones in a line on the fence,
bovine vertebrae after bovine vertebrae—
By walk away, I mean lead a dignified life—

Can Words Reach the Dead?

Catch up soon? I texted April—

CH'IXI

Certain folk shift the possible,
upend and refocus the gaze—

Ch'ixi, according to Silvia Rivera Cosicanqui, is:
a color that is the product of a juxtaposition, in small points
or spots, of opposed or contrasting colors... It is this heather gray
that comes from the imperceptible mixing of black and white,
which are confused by perception, without ever being completely mixed...
It is the logic of the included third... firewood that burns very fast—

Child: *I'm coloring into the night to make a beautiful drawing.*
The biggest one [referring to a paintbrush] *had to get the black up—*

CLOUDS ON THE FLOWERBED

Clouds are high-heeled, heavy—
Clouds carelessly collapse—
Covid walks down a city street—
Coyotes call—
Cry me a river, my mother says,
looking for dirt under her nails—

Dead

Cutting beets, I separate the whole
wheelbarrow full from their greens,
then load the huge heart-shaped bodies
into bags to give away—

Damaged by warfare—

Days a teapot makes an inconceivable beauty
out of nothing but steam in air—

Days ago, the hay smelled winy—

DITCH THE EMPIRE

Difference in melanin and territory colors us,
but no home is permanent—
Dinosaurs battled parasites, mosquitoes, meteors—
Divine violence?
Does every mother dream their child
absolutely, unequivocally needs
a bullet-proof vest?
Does the sky seem darker?
Don't shoot me, my pants are falling down—

Double Mask

Down the path the rain comes—
Dreams in which I swim under the water,
searching for holes in the ice—
End of tender underfoot—
Even the dead aren't safe—

THE WORLD'S FIRST SUICIDE BOMBER

Extensive bamboo pipelines
connected oil wells

to salt springs. It was back then,
in the era of the discovery of oil

and firepower, that the firebird flew.
Lit gunpowder packed into an apricot pit

served as its necklace. Shooed toward the enemy,
the bird landed on tree limbs. Imagine the explosion

of feathers, the sharp tang of sulfur, the sparks—

FATALLY KNEELING ON THE NECK OF

Feather fell
from the sky—
Felt so foreign—
Field mice rolled
in mud—
*Fighting would have
someone else killed*—
Filming—
Flowers stayed
up to worry—
For the disappearance
of themselves—

The Bereaved

From the Judge's Wig—
From the stone arch of the door—
Full moon pours—
Getting higher and higher up—
Getting lost in the air—
Gliding at angles of more than three feet forward, generating lift—
Gnats get all lovely; call them ghosts—
Gorgeous—
Goya, how did you paint that scene?
[With a] grubby hand?
Guidelines included *The Principles of Being a Good Neighbor*—

HALF-SPEECH SONG

He [Baghdadi] died after running into a dead-
end tunnel, whimpering and crying and screaming
all the way. He had dragged three of his young children
with him. They were led to certain death—

He [April's father] was a security guard—
He was napalmed—

Heartbreaking: the child marveling
at the 27 dollars in his purse tells me
that now he can afford his Covid vaccination
[blue band-aid under brown sweater]—

Her [April's mother's transplanted] heart—
Her [April's] small ears—
Her [April's] voice broken—
Her [Darnella Frazier's] young cousin
wearing a LOVE T-shirt—

Hercules slayed the guard of apples
that tasted of never-ending life—

Here, I am gutted—

How Much Detail to Give a Cloud

How can blood suddenly stop traveling
to one limb and fell my best friend?

How common such loss is—
How do we stomach all the punk?

I erect borderlines out of fear, mimicking
the territorial war of the fungi who leave

in their wake boundary lines of melanin
and pigment (black, brown, green, yellow, orange, red)

that glow with a brilliant, sometimes even neon color—
How quickly all we know can be extinguished—

How silent it is, watching the wake—
How to describe the extreme blue?

I Am a Mother

i am done with this dust—
I am not speaking
of me but of all mothers—

I Hear Cut Cedar Crying in the Far Field

I bend and pick, I sing, I gather—
I dream of April standing luminous before a hay field—
I fear for my son in this place where flags wave—
I feel something let loose inside me—
I find myself awake at night, the gentle owl of my heart
flapping in attempt to wake itself—
I have been showing my son the vanishing point—
I have to ask, *Did April die?* I have to ask—

Door of No Return

I may as well write: April,
killed by racism, age 38—

I Pass Women Sewing at their Singers and a Blind Albino Child

I once walked and ran great distances—

I once wanted to vanish—

I once wrote letters to a prisoner at Guantánamo. The letters always came back opened. One day, shortly after I interviewed the police chief (famous for fashioning the restraint chair prisoners are strapped into for force-feeding), I received a call. Someone on the other end laughed and then said they were calling from Guantánamo to order pizza—

I order White Supremacy Is Terrorism T-shirts—the shirt Patricia Okoumou wore on July 4, 2018, the day she scaled Lady Liberty armed with a modest proposal: *In a democracy, we do not put children in cages—*

I pee in the woods near deer droppings—

I pick ticks off the dog—

I plunge my hands in hot water, chop onions—

I pour water from one bucket to another; already the large bucket is empty—

I read of a man, released from Guantánamo, now raising pigeons—

I read of terrorist training cells—

I release the string to my son's flexible flyer and he's off, shrieking like I used to—

I remember all the places I had to journey to—

I remember as a child, melting snow off my mittens on a woodstove, and just how that snow sizzled. My son now does the same thing. Removes his gloves right over the iron surface on purpose. Snow from his gloves zigzags atop the black stove—

I remember my father running around with a tennis racket, chasing after a bat—

I remember the day my father handed me an article about human flying squirrels—

I remember talking with April—

I remember what it was like to think I was safe, that my dad could protect me—

I replay Darnella Frazier's video in my mind—

I run down the road clutching a jar of black currant jam—

I said stupidly to April: *I've had my heart do weird things—*

I see home in Horace Pippins' paintings. I'm thinking about the woods
where I was reared and what they did to me. I am walking in the dark—

I see now—

I sell $150 of ice cream by the end of the day. I'm the top seller. *High girl
of the day*, says George—

I sit at John Brown's farm. Brown never really lived here, and most Blacks
who settled here moved on. Brown, the white revolutionary, fancied himself
a *father* of freed men come to homestead. Look here at all that commemorates him
as contrasts what is left of my friend—

I sit on a pickle jar—

I speak to someone of not feeling safe. Flags flying correlate
with the absence of facemasks. How quickly the zoning changes,
how targeted we are—

I take a flower out of my son's bike chain and watch—

I tell him about the creaking gate, my dad in the ditch—

I tell my son a story now in which he and his friend flee
Trump supporters. They fly on magnetic brooms underground.
He and his friend's monkey chuck coconuts
at one Trump supporter who keeps shooting
the nuts until he is buried
in coconut water. I tell the tale as we drive past
the most rickety homes still flying Trump Rambo flags—

I think my son and I were shot at yesterday on the drive home. There is no other
sense to make of the sound so loud and close; no rock could have hit the car
with such force and not broken something. The crack must have been a bullet—

I think of April at the sink, untwirling her updo—

I think of X's bright shoelaces—

I think: as long as the walk-around my father cut through the wood exists
and my son walks it, he will be okay; my father's ghost will guide him—

I try to whisper to my son to look the other way—

I used to talk to April's mother—

I wake in the middle of the night and wonder who
the Uber driver was who ferried April—

I wake with these words for April—

I Watch Clouds Gather

I'm looking at a photograph of a bearded Romaine Tenney on his hay mower hitched to draft horses in a half-cut field. Tenney, whose Vermont farm was slated to be swallowed by Interstate 91, immolated himself, rather than be forcibly moved. My son says, *I may go off for an adventure, but I will always come back here!* He points to the ground. Tenney went off to war, came back. Didn't leave ever again. He was offered resettlement funds when the interstate was zoned, but what would such funds mean to someone partnered with a specific meadow? Our neighbor's barn is full of hay despite it having been inordinately wet—so wet mushrooms explode across the forest floor. Tiny fungi are probably sprouting in the hay bales, too. Meanwhile, chanterelles sit in wet towels in our fridge. Inside dead trees, fungi battle, erecting zone lines, secreting pigments of obnoxious hues. Such spalting is also evident in humans as differing skin, hair, and eye colors. Place colors us. Cornrows are canerows in the Caribbean. When I was growing up here in Vermont, kids used to close the bus windows whenever we passed The Stinky Farm. A boy named Cecil with an enormous cowlick in his sandy hair got on at that stop. I always envisioned the cows licking him. Tenney, even in arthritic pain, refused the electric milk machine neighbors tried to foist upon him. He milked by hand and let all his animals go before setting fire to his house with him in it. The rain is soft. I wish I knew where to put the grief. There is nothing; no gutter. Everything floods. The confusion is even nature's own. The earth's eminent domain is unarguable. She'll right herself, but will we? This summer my son and I built a paddock, felling dead trees for posts with a handsaw and an ax. That was when April called, out of breath. *Get a second opinion,* I told her. This was after April's mother died. April hadn't known what to do with her mother's house in a neighborhood that wouldn't give her its worth. She shopped, instead, for a security system. *We know 'homelessness' is a measure of belonging, not a lack of home ownership,* she once wrote. When forcibly removed from any real relationship with place, person, animal—who, then, are we, April?

I'm Not Forcing You to Watch

I'm remembering when April's mom gave April, who had no children of her own,
a Mother's Day card; this was back when April kept track of all her mom's meds, called
in prescriptions, and tried to get her to stop sneaking junk food, cigarettes

I'm SCARED wtf—

I've been reading April's emails, we exchanged thousands—

If injustice is essentially human—

If it wasn't for me 4 cops would've still had their jobs, causing other problems—

Illuminated shadow—

Gilled blots—

Inconceivable

In some cultures, the dead
are said to come back as clouds—
In suits of canvas, wood, silk,
steel, and even whale bone—
In the face of an automatic
or a rifle with a bump stock—
In the middle of a wood—
In the smoggy city center—
In the steel blue morning—

Hauled to Shore, Propped Up as Art

It is one-thirty in the afternoon—
It is pouring rain—
It isn't my child lying there—
It's water. *Hi cloud—*

Selling Mississippi Muds at Dusk

Jacob Blake, shot six times by police, paralyzed
from the waist down lies handcuffed
to a hospital bed. His dad: *He can't walk. Why handcuff him?*

Kids drop change in the window crack—

Killing insects is the only act of violence
that's never punished even within us—

Killing the black creature—

Later, a girl comes out from behind a fence with straightened hair
and asks me to help her figure out the change. She's gotten hung up
counting dimes and nickels. An old woman cries because she wanted
her strawberry dipper covered in peanuts. A lonely teen buys five
ice creams. *I knew the ice cream truck was coming today!*

Leaves breathe heavily—

Leaving behind—

On How the Police Bombed Tree's House on Osage

Light can fall so that one side
of an object is illuminated—
Light is left to grace us?
Light, unadulterated?

Like how the Supreme Court
determined that Sheriff Screws
had been under *the color of the law,*
despite the fact that Screws beat
a handcuffed Hall for at least
fifteen minutes? What the white court
meant was that Screws did not,
in other words, intend to deprive
Hall of his rights. Screws didn't mean
to kill him, even though it is said,
he carried a grudge and had threatened
that he would get Hall—

Like skateboarders push off the lip—
Listen. Sometimes my phone died—

Manumit from the Latin *Manumittere*: To Send Out from One's Hands

Living in a house my father built
by hand at the end of a dirt road—

Long distance friend: my red sled—
Lost in the air, ghosts show off

their scratches, tears—
LOVE waits, unseeing—

Making my child cry—
Man-made objects

are increasingly named after nature
and advertised as the real thing—

Many viruses take over cells
using genetic material to hijack them

to make new viruses—
Meanwhile my entire life

has been lived in light
of what some might call

humanity's suicide—
Meanwhile, jade pits rupture,

and miners die in the ensuing landslides—
Members of the jury: weigh in on the problem

of genre, as what's real is the base question—

MISDIAGNOSIS

Missing puzzle piece, my son says. He fiddles
with the Christmas lights; they blink—

Moses thinks our tissues are turning to stone—

Most of my father's ashes are scattered around
an old oak that is diseased and still stands—

Most of the souls are out in the open—

Moths' empty shells—

Mourners reach out—

MOVE bodies found in cardboard boxes
in academic labs; children's bones to teach what again?

MOVING THROUGH NETHER

Mushroom that dissolves itself
in just hours post-pick
pops up in the rain—

My brakes give out and I hit the back end
of a car in front of me at a red light. *They were cracked
in half*, The Pig tells me, looking at the brake pads
after taking the wheels off. *See how George runs this?*
The other woman's car isn't hurt. The truck's radiator,
however, is popped and now there's a small pond
in the middle of Swan Street. *One radiator has been in
fourteen different trucks*, The Pig says. *We repair them
all the time.* I fall asleep on top of the ice cream cooler—

My child jabs wool over and over,
fashioning a yellow song bird, until it is felt—
needled, made recognizable by repetition,
rhythm. *I could make anything*, he brags.
He keeps on jabbing, jabbing—

My child loses a milk tooth and there is no tooth
fairy, as I have no cash, so I keep the tooth—

My child puts a flashlight inside his mouth
and says, *I have such a hot cheek.* My hand sweats
over tea. The dog brings in a cow bone—

My child writes: *There is a pandemic and it is killing people*—

FAMILY PORTRAIT WITH THE MISSING

My father, kerosene lamp in hand, always put out
by nature, could be found perennially bent over,
fixing something. Porcupines ate the house, the underside
of the car, crazy for salt. My father stoned one—

My father's stone masonry partner made cheese. Beautiful
cheese covered in ash and flowers—

My grief coexists with the child stuffing his mouth with egg, zooming
his Lego creation around to his own sound effects, not to mention
the head of a giant dog in my lap together with the wood fire's warmth.
Grief would have us forget where we are and focus on an absent beyond.
But right here, at this instant, daylight not yet tickling the sky,
the child's limbs long, my coffee not yet lukewarm, here we are—

My head is the flag I raise—

My mother at 73 with a crowbar, out lifting stones from the earth. Four hours
of work only, she says. And then it got rainy and cold—

My mother comes from the garden, claw in hand—

My mother gardening naked, my own little crooked apple tree there
            by the clothesline—

My mother up in her house, drinking coffee—

My mother who picks up dead branches
and snaps them, before cradling them in her arms —

My parents and I lived on a road barren of contact—

My seven-year-old son is George Floyd—

My son and I look up at the stars. He wants to see Hercules, but the clouds are heavy. He gets cold. We go in. He reads a book in which round characters impersonate the planets. *Oh stop, stop, stop!* He laughs—

My son and I march around in white with other protesters—

My son and I visited April in Harlem the fall before Covid struck. The painting of flowers, *Say Her Name*, hung on her apartment wall—

My son and I walk and walk. Whenever we come across anything dead (mouse, worm, bird), we dig a hole for it—

My Son Hawks Handmade, Cardboard Phones—

My son is *eight becoming nine*—
My son lines up his toy cars, plays their sirens—
My son says: *You know they'll hunt me anyway*—
My son's soft cheek under apricot oiled hair—

My Video Went World Wide for Everyone to See and Know

Names? Too many dead—
Negative space—
Nether—
Never to be completely dark,
even were one to remove
the effects of starlight—

No Body

No return—
No savior—

Not on the horizon—
Not unlike the boat

that became art
in which so many
migrants drowned—

Nothing. You can do nothing,
Cyprian tells me. We stand
before a genocide memorial—

Now people in wingsuits,
human flying squirrels, glide—

Now the sumac turns black—

Marcescence

Of ash—
Of boatmen—

Of death and of what comes after—
Of doorposts—

Of everyone I cannot see—
Of late, there's been a fight over the old maple,

the last remaining marker of Tenney's farm
and, at one time, the farm's centerpiece. The tree,

ultimately, was felled, as the town feared
for the safety of those who parked their cars

(this part of the old farm is now a park
and ride) under it as it aged—

Of mostly found material:
to recall trauma—

Of Tomatoes in the Cellar, Red, Red

Of our kitchen; the squirrel I refuse to trap—
Of people getting Covid—
Of poem—
Of suspense. This gate that was built by my father to keep the hunters out—
Of the blood clot that would kill April inside an Uber?
Of the bungee-corded doors—
Of the day I sell $169; this means I bring home $40—
Of the dead?
Of the divide. I, too, wanted to watch TV as a child. Now, it is my son who begs—
Of the soul—

Often April's Cell Signal Was Scratchy

Old blue star so massive—

Old homeplace—

On a blue bench close to the pine-needled ground—

On a ladder, someone tends the memorial flame—

On a rock outside my father's old stone masonry shop,
my son and I flip through a book. *Since 1888, the earth has,*
I read, warmed the equivalent of an ice cube's melt. What were ice cubes
(when there were no ice cubes in actuality), I say, *are now puddles*—

On batteries, all lit up—

On earth as it is in heaven?

On horseback. Whoa—

[George] on how to rig an exhaust system: *There you go. An experience*
with The King. See how we did that? You saw what I handed him.
Davie, you're the best, man! Ten bucks every time I let him stick that
probe up my ass. Pretty funny, huh? It reads the adjustment, how much
to tighten it. See how we waltzed right through emissions? They all know
what's going on. The cops' problem is with me, not you. Remember that.

On July 4th, 2020, a year to the day before April died,
my son, his granny, and I picnicked unknowingly
at an environmental graveyard. I didn't think about the sign
on the rock near the road that read *Spirit Sanctuary.*
My son jumped down into an open grave, dug in the pine loam,
and it did, I thought then, look like a grave, and why was it here
in the middle of the forest? Pine needles floated into our lemonade—

On moss at John Brown's—

On my desk, behind an image of April and me, looking either like twins
or lovers, it's hard to say, is a drawing my son made when he was six
of chandeliers. I love the drawing—and I loved watching him draw it,
looking up. He surprises me often; his brilliance a deep well—

On my wall, a photo of my son—

On the forest path behind my pop's workshop where we live now—

On the phone when her [April's] mom had her clot—

Once April and I walked uphill from an ice cream store
through the Phoenixville cemetery, and sat in the roots
of the tree beside someone's wadded up paintball-stained clothes—

Once I said, *I don't know. Why try?*

Once upon a time I asked my father why—

Once upon a time my father called
to give me a play by play
of a meteor shower—

Once upon a time, a girl gave up writing
because she lacked the resources to fight
against an ever more corporate market
that controlled the movement of words.
The next day she came across Brecht's
wartime diary. In it, he wrote of this very idea
and she knew then that he was right
about fascism's existence in every age.
Words have always been marketed. They were,
some argue, invented to keep market-driven tabs—

Once April sat in my truck near the library. There was a trying of patience, by no means horrible. I remember words about woods and no speaking; a return to self, which meant a return to writing. She was crying because of the difficulty. Later she would write: *you, this woman, who always implored me to stay in the car/and let whatever fall, cry, be present/ do tell me your dreams/ i want to hear where you are located—*

One girl, scolded by her mother for not watching for cars, cries. A fourteen-year-old orders in a dust storm: *I haven't bought ice cream in so long. They don't have these kinds in stores.* I tell her I'll be back. She says, *Do, 'cause most ice cream truck drivers around here are crack dealers—*

One-eyed Amanirenas Fights with Her Son, Buries Augustus's Bust, and Keeps Rome at Bay

Onesimus didn't receive any applause
for sharing his knowledge of variolation
with witch-hunter Cotton Mather; no—

Onesimus ended up having to buy his freedom—

Only for the sake of the hopeless ones have we been given hope—

Only poetry is left and nothing possible anymore—

Only prehistory up there—

Only to become criminal slaves of the state—

or in the same position George [Floyd]...was in—

Organs—

Our ancestors could see through—

Our lives paper-thin—

Our molecular symmetry producing iron oxides—

Out of a tree, more rush of air than body—

Out of our longing—

Out, radiating—

Outlast us—

What It Means to Continue

Overcomes me
that I am sliding,
even as I sit—

Overshadows—

Paintings of animals
outlined atop and
slightly to the side
of one another,
shimmering in a dark
cave, lit by fire—

Paintings of plugs,
appliances. We eat by
candlelight—

Papayas mold—

Pasolini went to Africa
to feel better about himself.
He hated consumerism,
hated it in the absolute sense—

Pears Drop Off the Tree and Rot

People are dying!
People are named heroes. Some are
dead. Others, still alive, rise
to receive medals—
People grow rude, hitting and slapping—
People take Juice of the Small-Pox;
and Cutty-skin, and Putt in a Drop—

PERCUSSION TRAVELS AT WHAT SPEED BY WHAT CONDUCTOR?

Pepper—
Pepper—
Pepper—
Pepper—
Pepper—
Pepper—
Pepper—
Pepper—
Pepper—
Pepper—
Pepper—
Pepper—

ODE TO THE PEACOCK ROOM

Pippin used an iron poker
for a paintbrush,
burned wood—

Place souls in sand
and they stick
together—

Plants can distinguish
blue colors from red—

Plaque That Read Battle Now Reads Massacre

Plucked from a puddle
amidst bombed rubble—

Plug and feather that stone—

Poems live in space, spinning, blindfolded—

Poetry doesn't answer—

Polished for two years straight—

Pompeii: bear I bought
as a child with my own money—

Popping my son's locks
like April taught me—

Prisons planned according to data
that shows where Black boys
fail fifth grade in high numbers—

Pull in there—

Pump—

Pushing her glasses up, hand flat—

Ramona Africa still blames the capitalist system—

Redlining, pollutants, pipelines, interstates without exits—

Remains of copper in sockets—

Remember all the blood? Panthers shot in bed?
Malcolm X in the ballroom, twins in his wife's womb?

Replaced only by the faint sugary smell
of Queen Anne's Lace—

Requiring viewers grapple with the fact—

Resistance is a long fight—

Schoenberg's Painting of Mahler's Grave

She [April] knew this would happen—
She knew what was happening—
She longed for a child—
She lost it all to this nation—
She spoke of not being able to write—
She was the connoisseur of parsing light,
illuminating what wasn't seen—
She'd been seeking healthcare—
So the music reflects that—

ON THE COLOR LINE

So this one Black mama, her son gets killed
by the KKK, and she forgives the killer,
I tell my son. *And then think about Chauvin's mama—*
doesn't even say sorry to Floyd's family—

So, who cares, you don't bomb them,
you don't kill them, my son says
when I tell him about what happened
to MOVE—

Some bodies bleed—

Some fruit refuses gravity—

Sounds like lil' daggers, my son says, playing atonal chords
on his synthesizer. *Sounds like cutting swords, slicing against*
each other. I'll turn off the thing—

Spalt—perhaps from the Latin *spalato*, meaning split—

Still Life

Spore prints—

Spray paint on steel—

Symbolic Capital—a Collective
Understanding of Oneself as Honorable

Sumac berries stick around. Birds rely on such seeds to see them through a difficult winter. Sumac, too, clones itself underground, female to female, berry to berry—

Table that was my father's—

Taught him [my son] to believe in bugs, revere them—

Tenderheaded—

[T]hat is also a blackness—

That reads: *I poop on fascists*—

That same day, Open Arms, after being turned away by both Italy and Malta, docked in Spain with 60 rescued persons: *it is the duty of all of us, but especially the institutions, to continue doing this in all cases*—

That there is such certainty: we will die—

The bats were out this morning at 5:45; I walked through their flyway—

The big bomb shook the whole house up and stuff—

The bird, though, sings louder—

The black hole caught on film is, in fact, invisible—

The bungee hooks nip—

The cat's eyes glow in the headlamp. She yowls when she's lost. I yowl back. Early a.m. clouds visible as density, blackness upon blackness—

The challenge to remain loving continues—

The child and I read of bats needing homes, being chased, targeted, crushed, knocked down. We read of white-nose syndrome. We read of Four Bears with his *ruined face* double-crossed and angry at white men. This Hidatsa chief felled by smallpox on July 30, 1837—

The closeness of our friendship, April, seemed to account for the familiar, even when the familiar, its terminology, its color line was and remains loaded. We would check on one another. If you flew anywhere, I made you call or text when you landed. *The body itself is subject to being taken away, scratched out*, you wrote—

The clot in your leg traveled—

THE COLOR OF US

The concrete floor is too cold—

The condemned houses on Osage
rebuilt inadequately, residents
camped out at a wildlife sanctuary—

The contour of the day zigzags,
manic in its banality—

The days aren't enough
to support the nights—

The dead ant is larger than the live one,
and slightly discolored—

The dead come inside out of you—

The dead light up—

The debris' light appears to surround—

The disaster of it all—

THE DISTANCE LIGHT MUST TRAVEL

The disturbance of the cold—
The dog drinks with unslaked thirst—
The ferry has shutdown, the train
doesn't run here anymore—
The fig tree grows unabashedly—
The Fourth of July?
The freeing of slaves originated with a slap—
The ground heaves—
The gymnasts keep on twisting—
The head of a stone bird swivels—
The homeless sleep—
The image of a glowing donut shape—
The instability of cloud—
The kill shot—

THE KILLING OF THE TICK

The last beautiful thing—
The last poem—
The last text—

The leaves hang wet, forsaken—
The light a crazy yellow—
The machete's dull, but still glistens—

The man walking beside me is ancient—
The mask is damaged, its forehead gouged—
The matter we are made of—

The memorial flame—
The moon a red crescent—
The more butterfly-like Walter Benjamin felt

he became as a child, the more, he says, whatever butterfly
he chased took on the color of human volition. Capturing
the butterfly, he adds, was the price he had to pay

to regain human form—
The more statues are felled, the more flags are flown—
The only hope RJ Young, author of *Let It Bang*, says he has is

that people who don't look like one another
[aren't the same race] fall in love, become friends—
The only light comes from the passing headlights

of motorcycles—
The operation involved in the snipping of circuitry
requires use of a bicycle tool found at a dusty pump track. The fire

is a warm current. The child wiggles a dragon wing. The disturbance
of the cold settling in doesn't bother him—
The other day I read a bumper sticker on a truck

in front of us out loud to him: *Trump hates black people*—
The party to my far right is discussing which cell phone plan is best—
The photographer who shot Birdie Africa through the cop car window

in one over-exposed gasp thought he'd missed. What was riding
in that backseat? What wolf child, naked, without its mother?
The Pippin pepper sometimes bears a white fruit—

The police bombing of the Africa's row house started a fire
that ripped through the neighborhood; the Black mayor
of the city of brotherly love said, *Stop the burn*—

The police most definitely would've swept it under the rug—
The punctum—
The pup found a deer leg yesterday and ran with it

proudly. It was fresh. The hoof so perfect. *Why just cut
the legs off? What if we saw a human leg like this?* I asked my son—
The pup trespasses onto neighbor's land. The ditch is dark

and we tarry there. Look at the neighbor's old house
in ruin. *I'm so sorry. You had such a pretty home!* I stand at the hedge,
holding the dog by the collar, apologizing to the dead—

The red, white, and blue bomb—
The resources to fight—
The road weeps dust—

The rolls taste of the earth—
The room, trying to embody the music—
The same attitude, my son says—

The seeds are easy to dry in my kitchen—
The setting of the soul—
The shadow of a phoebe—

The sky spits its chew—
The smell of shoe polish overwhelms—
The song of boatmen rowing—

THE SOUND OF SIRENS

The spirit world as it overlaps the human—
The squirrel has eaten through the wall—
The stronger the soul, the stronger its cracks—
The suckers are stale and taste like kerosene—
The sumac turns red again—

THE SUMERIAN WORD FOR LETTER THE SAME AS THE WORD FOR STAR

The sun dribbles out across the lake—
The thirst of a plant—
The three-year-old hunchback—
The tick crawls upwards to the dog's head. We are forested—
The tiniest screw, as if to an eyeglass arm—
[T]he truth of what it is, or the reality
of what it was. Histories are written from a perspective—
The ululating—
The warming earth—
The wearing of black—
The whole world goes black—
The wind beats outside. Dionne Brand's voice grants permission.
She places bits next to bits. There is the collage of how
she is navigating the wake—
The witness, who just wanted to be shot, escaped
across a lake of floating bodies—
The woman whose car I hit didn't care about calling the cops. After the accident
we were both laughing and saying, *It's not funny.* She cleans houses for a living.
Shit happens, she said. Her car she told me was spotless before she moved here
from Florida. Now there's a crack in the windshield, a scrape on the door, and
the new edition: two puncture marks in the cover to the spare that saved her
car's back end from the front of my truck—
The wooden fence rail—
The world smushes [child's hands ball] *and it will unfold—*

Bats

Their quirky movements
part of some larger
crepuscular language—

These Are the Backwards Days

There is currently no point
around less than four miles
from a road. Wildlife corridors
are being fashioned out of blocks
of private land to protect species
whose habitat is severely fractured
by human encroachment—

There is nothing else to say—

There is only pain, only—

There was a statue of a vigilante
on a horse who cut off young
Indigenous men's feet. Someone cut
off the statue's bronze foot—

There was also my father's death
and my son's arrival—

They say, *Baghdadi was using his two children
as human shields—*

*They were using the children
to appeal to our humanist sensibilities,*
Philly's police chief argued—

Thinking of performance, of grieving—

This is the time to cry to the heavens, to hide
in caverns. Will we emerge? Behind me
my son plays with Legos. [Sound effects of explosions]—

THROMBOSIS

[T]o abjure grief or rage... Refusing,
like Walter Benjamin, to accept
the linear ravages of history, taking in the ruin—

To be alive on others' bones—

To build a bunker that withstands a rain of fire—

To give back all that was stolen—

To remember anything—

To the grand narrative that is myth—

To the raccoons tipping over the chicken food—

Together, alone—

Tomato stems encircled in string, so as to raise them up—

Tomorrow we will continue to say good-bye, Alfred says, rifling
through photographs of the dead—

Tomorrow We Will Continue to Say Goodbye

[T]oward the sun as the true picture
of the past whizzes by. Such is the necessity
to take control of memory as it flashes
in a moment of danger—

Traffic is bad and my son predicts
that a deer has been hit on the road—

COLLECTIVE POEM

Trump calls the Belgian Malinois, slightly injured
by Baghdadi's blast, *a dog, a beautiful dog, a talented dog.*

Truth hunted, detained, killed by the government—

Truth is not some private discovery or individual experience.
The truth of existence takes place through communication...
a communication of being, such that being itself is shared
interpretively, reality-through-communication—

Turns grey with rot from rain—

A Photo with April

Two girls (one in leotard and tights,
the other in a satin nightgown) strike
poses. Note their perfect postures
as everything around them collapses—
Two high-pitched coos—
Two little bat phones—

On Driving an Ice Cream Truck

Vito about ice cream and its appeal:
You can tell me what time, and I'll tell you
what street I'm turning down and which way
I'm looking. Just think: You're in a Santa suit.
You're a hero. After a while, when you become
part of the neighborhood, you become invisible—

Vito about ice in the cooler
where the pop for sale is kept: *Water the ice.*
Water it again. That way the ice gets in the small places,
wiggles in. Then fill it up with ice again. Smash up
the dry ice into a powder and spread it. It will seal it
in there. There's an art to sloping the ice and not cracking
the hinges off your cooler, even when you purposefully fill it too full.

Vito: *I'm not even first generation yet. My mother and father were*
in the United States, in New Jersey, for only four days when I was born.
My mother died giving birth to me. My father was found with her body
and deported. He was wanted in Italy because he was a Communist.
He was assassinated when I was four. I was on the boat. I remember
the explosion. They said he was killed, but my uncle told me otherwise.
I was taken to a rectory. You know what that is? Then my uncle
in the States sent for me. I trained as a boxer. Was disqualified in a fight.
I kicked this guy's neck—

WALK WITH PIGEONS

Watching the clouds roll in—
Waterlines: what wood turners first called spalt—
Wave wildly. The dead—
We all wait, marooning—
We are made bare before vultures—
We are the buriers, we chant, *of the dead*—
We can't all be heroes, Cyprian says—
We cross the road and walk on a path, past doorways of empty houses—
We have traded in love for the traffic of blood—
We live in the sticks, in country teeming with deer racks—
We move across the lake, leaving one side behind—
We must go nonviolently rogue—
We need jade to counteract the iron-quartz effect—
We need more than augury—
We now know what the jury decided—
We park the trucks in the garage—
We pass blood-smeared tarmac and see the deer's body roadside—
We pour out of the gates and down the streets in a slow, coagulated stream—
We wanted to ride bikes and watch TV like other kids (Birdie's small voice)—
We write cards my son can hand out: *Stop staring. Don't talk to me about my hair*—

WHAT IS SPIRITUAL AND FINE

Were the children, the white questioner asked, *hostages?*

What a death knell as contrasts my memory
of our wind-up record player: Fat Albert slowing down
as the crank slowed, my father's laughter, the grass
we lay upon—

What can be said? Death eviscerates the thrumming of us, April—

What can I say? I try to write. I erase—

What can we learn from viruses? *There is no us and them—*
just a gradually blending and shifting mix of DNA—

What do I do with these letters that will never reach you, April?

What do we do with the love all the way through? *Bathometer,*
my mom says, speaking of measuring the depth of the lake
we cross; four hundred feet here, at its deepest point—

What does it mean that everything keeps barreling on?

What does it mean to return to a mother who still gardens?

What does it mean to save a fly from a bucket of water? To build
a bunker that withstands a rain of fire? To hunker in a basement
living out one's faith that freedom is a moral ground?

What happens to the soul then amongst all the endless color?

What Have I Done Oh Lord, the name of an ox 4,000-years-old—

What I see is terror. What I see in myself is terror. I see it as I yell
at my son, as I attempt to warn him of the dangers—

What is spiritual or fine cannot be enjoyed out in the cold
on concrete pilings. The song of the earth blows kisses.

What is the grainy video of Baghdadi's compound exploding?
What am I looking at? Why? Why? Why? Why? Cradling my head
and not understanding who we are, what species—

WHERE LIGHT AND DARK REMAIN

What Marxists are fighting for are the basic necessities
without which nothing spiritual or fine can be enjoyed,
and this is what turns us, heliotropically—

What she [April] called (and didn't have), *The good insurance—*

What to the slave is—

What's left is a slave language danced with blades—

When April dies—

When has low iron translated into an absence of breath?

When I was a child my father photographed me
bathing my white doll beside a Black friend
bathing her Black doll in a bathroom sink—

When I was my son's age, my parents made a wattle fence
for a goat and sheep that promptly escaped. I preferred
to watch *Guiding Light* down at the neighbor's. My parents were sweaty,
muscled beings, and I was in public school, a kid reared off-grid—

When I was my son's age, we hit a bump on South Road—

When my father would fling me—

When the cheese was cut—

Where I planted flowers—

Which is really whiteness not being able to handle its far-flung torture;
whiteness, not being able to look back—

Why Try? I Once Asked

Why try? April echoed—
Why try? April echoed—
Why try? April echoed—

WITH THE UNLIVABLE

With a hysterectomy, even though—
With blades, bones—
With her [April's] mother's house—
With steel wool scrubs—
[W]ith the unlivable, becoming 'coeval with the dead,' refusing—
Wood turners inject their spalted turnings
with cactus juice to preserve them—
Word made rag—
Words are being outlawed—
Words made of space—
Words thrown around—
Works she [April] didn't cotton to—
Worth of ice cream (an old woman tells me there are no children
in the neighborhood, when, in fact, four stand around my truck)—
Wounds reopen, wounds thought cauterized—
Write: *killed*—

X's Bright Shoelaces

X'ed—

Dear April,

You rarely spoke in a way that would be called direct. Enjambment
got you. You once said you wrote not out of inspiration but
endurance, and this muscle, I wager, is what gave you the pluck
to remain friends with me. I'm not easy. Some days you would get off
the phone feeling sick. I, too, got worked up. We rallied. And, after
more than a decade, it mattered that we rallied. There was history. You made me
a sugar bowl; the clinking was a spoon stirring the sugar in. I made you
planets of blue that chipped and rotted. Words without end—

You wrote: *mourning is a state devoid of a compass—*

You'll survive, you said
when my father was dying,
your father already dead.
I told you to make your poems
a memorial to your mother,
when you stopped writing
after she died—

Your light so bright you almost glared, glasses all shiny,
hair plastered back in braids, hand in front of your mouth
as if to block what might slip out—

Your number in my phone appears as *a.*

Unattributed Quotes

5   *Don't be dead I love you so:* John Ronsheim's translation of concluding scene in Arnold Schoenberg's opera *Erwartung*; could also be translated, *Don't be dead, my lover.*

5   *A brokenness that is also a blackness:* Jack (also Judith) Halberstam in intro to Fred Moten and Stefano Harvey's *The Undercommons: Fugitive Planning and Black Study.*

6   *Go and tell the world what you have seen:* Ben Okri.

7   *a nis place, really nis. Trees grow:* André Ulmer.

18   *Don't shoot me, my pants are falling down:* Birdie Africa during the bombing of MOVE bunker.

19   *Even the dead aren't safe:* Walter Benjamin.

21   *Fighting would have someone else killed:* Darnella Frazier texted (after being accused of filming not giving aid to George Floyd).

22   *The Principles of Being a Good Neighbor:* MOVE guideline.

23   *He died after running into a dead-end tunnel, whimpering and crying and screaming all the way. He had dragged three of his young children with him. They were led to certain death:* Donald Trump.

25   *i am done with this dust:* Lucille Clifton.

32   *I'm not forcing you to watch; I'm SCARED wtf; If it wasn't for me 4 cops would've still had their jobs, causing other problems:* Darnella Frazier, see note for page 23.

35   *Killing insects is the only act of violence that's never punished even within us:* Elias Canetti.

36   *Light can fall so that one side of an object is illuminated:* Okobong Nkanga.

40   *My head is the flag I raise:* April Freely.

43   *My video went world wide for everyone to see and know:* Darnella Frazier, see note for page 23.

50   *Only for the sake of the hopeless ones have we been given hope:* Theodor Adorno.

50   *Only poetry is left and nothing possible anymore:* Pier Paolo Pasolini.

50   *or in the same position George…was in*: Darnella Frazier, see note
      for page 23.

52   *People take Juice of the Small-Pox; and Cutty-skin, and Putt in a*
      Drop: Onesimus.

60   *symbolic capital—a collective understanding of oneself as honorable*:
      Zakiyyah Iman Jackson.

60   *it is the duty of all of us, but especially the institutions, to continue*
      doing this in all cases: Barcelona mayor Ada Colau.

60   *The big bomb shook the whole house up and stuff*: from Birdie
      Africa's testimony after bombing of MOVE.

68   *the truth of what it is, or the reality of what it was. Histories are*
      written from a perspective: Okobong Nkanga.

71   *to abjure grief or rage… Refusing, like Walter Benjamin, to accept*
      the linear ravages of history, taking in the ruin: Yogita Goyal.

72   *toward the sun as the true picture of the past whizzes by. Such is*
      the necessity to take control of memory as it flashes in a moment of
      danger: Walter Benjamin.

73   *Truth is not some private discovery or individual experience. The*
      truth of existence takes place through communication… a
      communication of being, such that being itself is shared
      interpretively, reality-through-communication: Sam Mickey.

77   *Were the children hostages?* from MOVE trial transcripts.

77   *There is no us and them—just a gradually blending and shifting mix*
      of DNA: Carl Zimmer.

79   *What Marxists are fighting for are the basic necessities without*
      which nothing spiritual or fine can be enjoyed, and this is what
      turns us, heliotropically: Walter Benjamin.

79   *What to the slave is*: Frederick Douglass.

81   *with the unlivable, becoming 'coeval with the dead,' refusing*: Yogita
      Goyal.

81   *Word made rag*: Walter Benjamin.